Ian Maclaren

Companions of the Sorrowful Way

Ian Maclaren

Companions of the Sorrowful Way

ISBN/EAN: 9783743308992

Manufactured in Europe, USA, Canada, Australia, Japa

Cover: Foto ©ninafisch / pixelio.de

Manufactured and distributed by brebook publishing software (www.brebook.com)

Ian Maclaren

Companions of the Sorrowful Way

Contents

	PAGE
Concerning the Way Itself	11
The Three Intimates of Jesus	29
The Owner of Gethsemane	47
The Bearer of Christ's Cross	69
A Noble Lady	89
The Daughters of Jerusalem	109
A Malefactor	129
A Roman Officer	151
The Funeral of Jesus	167

Concerning the Way Itself

Concerning the Way Itself

NO one can have any doubt where the Way ended, but he may have two minds as to where the Way began. If life is to be judged rather by its general trend than by the acute experience of a few hours, then it should never be forgotten that all His days the Man of Sorrows was carrying His burden. If life, on the other hand, be estimated not by the running of a sand-glass, but by the beating of the heart, then surely our Lord endured more cruel agony on His last day than in all His years. There was the unseen Cross of divers afflictions, which rested on His life and weighed down His soul from the cradle to the Upper Room, and this was a sore discipline; and there was the visible cross of two rough beams which was laid upon His bleeding shoulders and weighed His body to the ground; and this was the symbol of an unspeakable tribulation. There were the clouds, which from early morning flecked the sky of our Master's life, and there was the black massy storm which at the last burst on His head. As the devout Christian chooses, he may join himself to the Lord in the Sorrowful

The Sorrowful Way

Way at Gethsemane, or three and thirty years earlier at the manger of Bethlehem. And it may not be unprofitable for the disciple to remind himself that the Lord was walking in the Sorrowful Way before the Incarnation, as He suffered and sorrowed over backsliding Israel unto bitter crying and lamentations, and that He is still to be found therein, as He shares from day to day the temptations and griefs of His Church.

Many happy days of childhood He must have lived at home with His holy Mother in the mountain village of Nazareth, amid the woods, and flowers, and fields, and animals which He loved. Yet the pain of self-repression is already

His, and the moan of the offended little ones is heard in His after-speech. Some quiet years of manhood He also spent at the carpenter's bench, where He was baptised into the toil of the world before he was baptised into its sin, and in the peasant life, whose ways were to run for ever through His parables. Yet it is evident from His discourses that He had tasted the weariness of labour and had been partaker of the unjust lot of the poor. Outside Nazareth His path, after a brief sunshine, lay in ever deepening shadows. People followed Him in crowds only to leave Him in displeasure. He called twelve disciples, who pained Him daily by their slowness

The Sorrowful Way

of understanding. In one village He was able to heal a few sick; in the next He could do nothing because of the people's unbelief. When He made His appeal to the good folk they suspected and misunderstood Him. When the publicans and evil-livers came to Him it was a cause of offence. One of His chosen band was a traitor, and there was not one on whom He could rely. No servant of His has ever fulfilled a harder ministry than the Master: from Capernaum to Jerusalem — lonely, rejected, disappointed, grieved — He walked in the Sorrowful Way.

The devout soul will not fail to see already the print of the nails on the paths of Galilee, or to hear the sighing of Jesus' heart as He spake in the synagogues; but the Church will ever count the last day of His life the sum of sorrow, and, although she may not always have the pictures before her eyes, she has ever the Stations of the Cross in her heart. As a vine through the long summer time drains its sap into the grapes, and in autumn the purple clusters are trodden in the wine-press, so was Jesus' life pressed into the Cup of Salvation, and the world has drunk of its sweetness. Sorrow having followed this Man all His days, now prepared her crown and set it on His head, and of all the ruby gems not one was wanting.

The Sorrowful Way

He was betrayed by one disciple, denied by another, and forsaken by all. He was despised by His nation, cast out by His Church, condemned by His rulers, refused justice by the Romans; He was counted a deceiver of the people, a rebel against law, a blasphemer against God. He was arrested, bound, scourged; He was spat upon, mocked, crucified. Having endured huge pains of soul and body, it seemed as if God Himself had forsaken Him, and after this fashion He travelled the Sorrowful Way.

As the Race once walked with God amid the trees of Eden, and after a long journey will at last come into the place where is the tree of life, with its twelve manner of fruits and its leaves for the healing of the nations, it was fitting that like human life, the Way should begin and end in a garden. First there is the garden of Gethsemane, where Jesus had His oratory and met with God, and the angels of God ministered to Him; and there is the garden of Joseph, where Jesus had His bed-chamber and those whom He had saved laid Him to rest, and He slept in peace after His sore travail. Between the two gardens the Way compassed all the varieties of life: in the valley of Kedron and on the hill of Calvary; in the country with its vines and olives, in the

The Sorrowful Way

city with its streets and crowds. Before He left the city, Jesus had been in a king's palace, and an ecclesiastical court, and a judgment hall, and a barracks. He was with kings, priests, governors, soldiers; He was with women, country folk, working people, malefactors. For the Way of Sorrow passes through all classes, all houses, all places, and therein Jesus walked from end to end, so that at whatever point one stands he may find himself with Jesus.

Between the way of this last day and the way in which Jesus had walked all His days, there remains this difference, that while before Jesus was chiefly active,

Companions of

now He is nearly passive. For three years He preached the Evangel in the synagogues, by the well-side, in boats moving gently upon the waters of the lake, on the grassy slope of hills. Now He holds His peace, and will answer nothing. Day and night had He laboured, journeying from city to city, untiring, self-forgetful, eager. Now He is led backwards and forwards at the pleasure of His guards. His joy before was to heal the sick, to raise the dead, to comfort those who mourned. Now His great power is hindered and sleeps as He Himself is smitten and wounded. Once His work was to gather disciples to His

The Sorrowful Way

side and instruct them in the mysteries of God's kingdom. Now, His desire is to secure their safety, and to see them depart in peace. For a lifetime He had set Himself to do the will of His Father, for the last day He resigned Himself to bear the same will, which was ever blessed and ever good.

If it were given unto us to choose the way wherein we should walk, is there one of us would not prefer the way of doing to the way of suffering? What soldier would not rather charge on the most forlorn hope, with an almost certainty of dying in the breach, than stand on the deck of a sinking vessel till she made the last plunge, and the cold waters closed over his head? For he who charged had done something; putting heart into an army, showing the road to victory, giving his body for a bridge; but he who stood did nothing, striking no blow, advancing no cause, leaving no memorial. What mother is there whose heart is not light as she watches over her children and toils for their welfare unto the hours of the night, but who would fret and worry were she laid aside and commanded to rest? Any servant of Christ would ten times rather face a hostile world even unto death in the declaration and defence of the Evangel, than be silenced and hear from afar the

The Sorrowful Way

sound of the battle. Ah! the multitude of victims who have ceased to labour or to resist, who carry the cross in silence and patience along the Sorrowful Way with the Lord.

It seems to sight an immense tragedy; but is it certain that the lives of victims are wasted, — rendering no service to God's good cause, having no share in the victory of the ages? It is not given unto us to know which has done most for a household; the strong man who won for them the meat which perisheth, by the sweat of his brow, or the gentle sufferer whose grace made clean their souls. We value highly the patriot whose brave words and stalwart heart establishes righteousness in the market-place, but may assign too little effect to his fellow held in prison and in bonds. When some ancient tyranny comes crashing to the ground, the reward will be divided between the soldiers and the martyrs. When for thirty-three years Jesus did the will of God most diligently, the world saw an example of perfect law-keeping, and now the child and the man, the sinner and the saint, all men and women together stand before God complete in His perfect obedience. So much He did for us and the eternal law in His lifetime. When for a single day Jesus meekly drank the cup His Father placed in His hands, He

The Sorrowful Way

broke the dread power of Sin, that in Him we all might stand victorious. So much He did for us and the eternal law in His Passion. The Sorrowful Way became the Sacra Via of triumph wherein He walked in white embroidered with purple and was not without His spoils; and the Cross to which He was nailed became His Throne.

The Three Intimates of Jesus

The Three Intimates of Jesus

ALTHOUGH it may be given unto the devout heart to enter into certain of the Lord's sorrows there are others which even St. John or Mary of Bethany can only see from afar. When His fellow-townsmen would have taken His life, or Pharisees from Jerusalem dogged His steps, or the foolish multitude wearied of Him, or even Judas Iscariot sold his Master for thirty pieces of silver, the vexation is within our understanding. When Jesus withdrew into the shadow of the olive trees and threw Himself upon the ground, and besought His Father time after time for relief, and sweated great drops of blood in His agony, the tribulation is beyond what even chief saints can think. Every sensitive nature must have moments of utter horror, when the naked shape of some loathsome sin is forced upon their gaze and they cry out in their outraged purity. Yet the finest nature is callous beside the soul of Christ, and its purity is black beside His whiteness. When therefore the sin of the race into which He had been born, and whose lot He chose to share, came to a climax in Jesus'

The Sorrowful Way

rejection and betrayal; when our rebellion, unbelief, cruelty; our selfishness, pride, treachery; our hatred, envy, falsehood — all the impieties of all the members of the Body — came upon Him, the Head, then His strength was nigh unto the breaking, and He shrank from the cup.

If any one be called unto Gethsemane he must leave his nearest intimates and drink this cup alone. In the supreme temptations and sorrows of life the soul is isolated, and it were unbecoming and impious that any human eye should peep upon its agony. Yet even in that awful privacy, when God's hand leads us into the secret place of grief and curtains us with darkness, we hunger for human sympathy, and we are disheartened if there be none to feel with us. One is comforted to know that near by a brother man is praying for him and waiting till haply he be delivered from his straits. Jesus was intensely human, and although He had spent many nights alone in this Garden in communion with the Father, He could not do without fellowship when He wrestled with temptation. He called aside His three intimates in the college of Apostles and led them to the verge of the great mystery. They were chosen to be companions. Some came of their own accord into the Sorrowful Way, as that young man

The Sorrowful Way

in the linen cloth, and Pilate's wife; some were dragged into this Way by the violent hands of men, such were Simon the Cyrenian and the penitent thief; some found themselves in the Way by the accident of circumstances — of them were the daughters of Jerusalem and the Roman centurion — but certain were summoned directly by the Lord to join Him at the very beginning of His Way, St. John and St. James, the two sons of Zebedee, and St. Peter.

If the Apostles be taken to represent the Church, then the Three stand for that inner circle of choice souls who chiefly understand the mind of the Lord, who chiefly feel with His heart. One was the type of vision, to whom the very heaven would yet be opened; one was the type of action, who should declare Christ's name before councils; one was the type of heroism, who first of the Apostolic band was to seal his testimony with his blood. They were the spectators of Christ's most wonderful works, the witnesses to His glory, the companions of His Passion. When Jesus called back Jairus's little maid from the dead by His kindly word, they stood beside the couch. When the veil between the seen and unseen dissolved, and Jesus' garments shone white as no fuller on earth could white them, they were on the Mount; when He

The Sorrowful Way

drank the bitter cup of this world's sin they saw His hands tremble at the lifting thereof. He is your intimate to whom you turn in the solemn moments of life, and this was the honour set by Jesus on the three Apostles.

Friendship can never be judged amid the ordinary circumstances of life — when we nod to our friend as he hurries past, when we are silent to him for months, when we chide him for some fault, when we give him careless advice. Friendship is proved when he is in the big black straits of life, and we remember nothing save our loyalty and his need. If three keep guard beside a man in his Gethsemane he is not to be pitied,

Companions of

but the friends in whom Jesus put His faith watched for a while and then slept. The sleep of the Three is the shame of the Gospels, and there be some to whom the failure of St. John is sadder than the Crucifixion. The people left Jesus, they were ignorant; the Pharisees slandered Him, they were bigots; Judas betrayed Him, he was a knave; Pilate crucified Him, he was a place hunter; for each an excuse can be found by charity. If even the eight slept, they were not His intimates. "Betrayest thou the Son of Man with a kiss?" was a keen reproach, but there was in it no complaint like this, "Could ye not watch with Me one hour?" It was the

The Sorrowful Way

cry of a wounded heart which in its hour of need had trusted its friends and been disappointed. When St. John could not keep vigil during his friend's hardest hour, although Jesus used no upbraidings but found a kindly reason in the weakness of the body, the nails of the Cross could not have been so bitter an affliction.

The Church will ever make her pious pilgrimage to the Garden of the Lord's Passion, and under the shadow of the olives she will ever learn the secret of sacrifice, for the Lord has not yet abandoned Gethsemane. While His flesh and blood throughout the world and in all ages endure cruel wrong and suffering, He cannot be indifferent or untouched. The far distance of heaven does not dull His ear to the crying of His kinsfolk, nor does the glory of the Father blind His eyes to the martyrdom on earth. Into His heart is all sorrow poured in virtue of His holy Incarnation and eternal Priesthood. The battlefields soaking with the blood of His brethren; the shameful wrongs of women and children; the sufferings of the prisoners who have done nothing amiss; the hunger and oppression of the poor; the torture of the dumb animals, which have no appeal except to their Lord, are His present Gethsemane. His is an

The Sorrowful Way

eternal passion, and a cup still refilled from day to day.

With the Lord is joined in this ministry of sympathy a band of companions who are the flower of the Church, and who have not slept on their watch. They are His chosen friends, and belong to all times and creeds and callings and countries — being as different one from another as St. John was from St. Peter, and finding their unity in the vision of the Master beneath the olives with His agonised prayer and His sweat of blood. Some are missionaries of the Lord, who bore the Cross in their hearts rather than in their hands, from St. Paul who poured out life as a drink offering, and Xavier, who

Companions of

stretched out his hands to the East and prayed for more sufferings — unto that pure spirit Brainerd, who grasped for multitudes of souls among his loved Red Indians, and Livingstone, who in his patience and charity carried the light of the Divine Love into the dark places of the earth. Some are lovers of their fellow men, such as that heroic monk, who, by an impulse of sacrifice, brought to an end the gladiatorial conflicts, and St. Vincent de Paul, with his devotion to the slaves of the galleys; such as Howard, who reformed the prisons of Europe, and Elizabeth Fry, who carried the Evangel to the prisoners. Some are rather deliverers and reformers and patriots and

The Sorrowful Way

martyrs, like John Huss and Hugh Latimer and Lord William Russell, and that modern knight-errant, General Gordon. They kept their vigil carefully, and drank Christ's cup without complaining, and filled up what remained of His sufferings for the salvation of the world.

What the Lord's companions have suffered with Him cannot be imagined by those of us who are of the outer circle. Theirs was not a passing feeling of kindly pity, nor the service of a few empty hours. They tasted the actual pain of the victims; they surrendered the tenderest joys of life; they strained their very reason in the keenness of their sympathy; they counted not their life dear in their

Companions of devotion. The world's sorrow has so overcome certain pious and sensitive natures that in their measure they also have besought God that the cup might pass. This has been their trial and this has been their strength. In this secret fellowship with the Man of Sorrows they were thoroughly cleansed from that unconscious callousness of heart which affords an inglorious security against the appeal of suffering, and that secret taint of selfishness which, as by an instinct safeguards our personal interests. It is in this travail of soul over the world that saints are formed and reach the heights of holiness: it is in this shadow that pious hearts are led into the mys-

The Sorrowful Way

teries of the soul and into the secret things of God. The agonies of life grow luminous and beautiful to those who are taken apart and who keep watch with the Lord.

It is not by the way of learning but by the way of suffering that we come unto knowledge, and he was right who, being asked how he came to know so much, pointed to the crucifix. They who sail on the surface of a summer sea gain no treasures, but they who, weighed down with sorrow, fear not to sound the depths, return to the light with pearls in their hands. One vigil in Gethsemane with Christ teaches more than can be heard in all the synagogues, than all we gather in our pleasant

The Sorrowful Way

days. We learn at last to say, "Thy will be done," and to make our final surrender; and if it be that hearts pass through misery's presses, heaven is already bending over us in benediction, and the angels of God are making haste to be our ministers.

The Owner of Gethsemane

The Owner of Gethsemane

AMONG the vivid scenes of our Lord's life His arrest in the Garden of Gethsemane is the most weird, and various circumstances fascinate the imagination. The moon filled the open glades with silver light, but underneath the trees the darkness hung heavy. Within an olive grove the Apostles lay huddled in a heap upon the ground, and a short distance farther the Lord prays alone. The stillness of the Garden is cut by a thrice repeated cry of agony, but no sound comes from the guilty city which lies in sleep, and in the awful light of judgment. Jesus wakes His friends and gathers them round Him in the shadows. A band of soldiers led by a guide comes cautiously up the open way; they peer into the gloom beneath the trees, flashing light from their lanterns; the Master comes forth undismayed, and Judas kisses Him in token that this is the man. There is a confusion of figures and clashing of arms, during which St. Peter strikes with the sword, and then Jesus is led away a prisoner, through the Garden where, night after night, He had spoken with God.

The Sorrowful Way

Before the excited company — among whom Jesus alone possessed his soul — had escaped from among the trees with their mysterious shadows, some one, glancing fearfully round, discovers that they are followed. A figure in pure white flits among the trees, appearing and disappearing, as if keeping watch and yet desiring to be unnoticed. As one after another catches sight of this ghostly attendant a vague fear spreads through the band. It was an eerie expedition and every incident was strange. They had been gathered suddenly at the Temple and set out under secret orders. They had crept through the midnight streets of Jerusalem like thieves, guarding against the rattle of arms and speaking each man with his neighbour in a whisper. They were led by a stranger, who seemed ill at ease and half repentant of his work. They were going to lay hands on Jesus, and round this Man there gathered a certain indescribable divinity. They trembled in the silence and moonlight of the Mount of Olives; and at the sight of Jesus coming out from the trees, and looking at them with those eyes, some strong men had fallen to the ground. They had come on ill-omened work, and now what meant this sight as if a corpse had risen from the dead to be a sign to them?

The Sorrowful Way

Some soldiers, braver than their fellows, spring suddenly aside and catch the whiteness, to find the under garment of a man left in their grasp, while its owner — his naked body glistening in the light — plunges into the wood and vanishes.

Amid the dramatic events which were to fill the next twelve hours this slight incident would be soon crushed out of the soldiers' minds, but it was treasured by one spectator, and at last found its place in the history of the Passion. No one in the Gospels made so brief and strange an appearance, a mere flash of white from darkness to darkness, and our curiosity is fired. Can this young man be identified, who, being no Apostle and having no invitation to the Garden, rose from his bed and haunted the very place where Jesus was praying?— who did not lose heart of a sudden and forsake his friend when even St. John and St. Peter had escaped for their lives; who could not resist the attraction of love and the desire to be with Jesus whithersoever He went; who hung upon the outskirts of the band and only fled when rough hands woke him into self-consciousness and outraged his modesty. This was not a coward, else he had gone with the Apostles: he was rather a lover and a recluse.

Was there any one among Jesus'

The Sorrowful Way

private friends who was likely to have been present that night of his own part, because he knew Jesus would be in the Garden, and because he also knew every recess of the Garden? What about the owner of Gethsemane? We read in the Gospels that after Jesus had spoken with the people in the Temple, and they had gone every one to his own house, He left the hot, noisy, restless city and spent the night on the Mount of Olives. Jesus had various homes, beneath whose kindly roof He could rest, but He loved the open air, and so it came to pass that He had the use of two gardens. One was that in which He slept well after the battle had been fought, and the owner thereof was Joseph of Arimathæa. The other was that which was an ever ready and welcome sanctuary for the Lord when He was worn out and sick at heart through the gainsaying and vain ambitions of men, and the owner thereof, was it not a certain young man?

If His nation was misled, and rejected Christ, how many were the kindnesses He received of His friends, and none could have been more grateful than the affording of this garden. It is good to feed them that are ready to perish and to send light to them that sit in darkness, but finer gifts still remain. Bread is good and knowledge is better, but best of all is peace, and the place of quietness has ever been and ever will be a garden. What wiser and kindlier gift could any one make to his brethren who are compelled to live amid the pressure and publicity of the city, where one is hardly allowed to possess his own soul, and oft-times has not a solitary place wherein to weep, than a sheltered place with trees and flowers? Temptations could be overcome and perplexities would unravel themselves and sorrows be comforted and the will of God grow luminous where the noise of the city is stilled and heaven is near. One day this young man, having come in from the Mount of Olives to hear his friend speak in the Temple, and standing in his shyness on the edge of the crowd, saw even at that distance the weariness on Jesus' face, and there came to him a gracious inspiration. When the crowd, discussing and wrangling, had dispersed, and the last scribe had left Jesus alone, His friend approached and made a simple request that the Master would come with him. They passed swiftly through the streets, where the people stood in groups, and up the side of Olivet in silence — for they were not mere acquaintances who are obliged to talk. They came at last into the garden and stood in its heart, and the young man found words to plead that if Jesus counted him

The Sorrowful Way

a friend, He would make this place His own. So it came to pass that if for Jesus there was no room in palaces nor great men's houses He had His home, the fairest on earth, beside which carved ceilings and many coloured curtains are less than nothing and vanity; where the morning light turned the grey olive leaves into silver and the birds settling down into their nests at evening spoke of their Father's care; where the gentle rustling among the leaves at noon was as the movements of the Divine Spirit, and the lilies in the glades bore witness to the gratuitous magnificence of God. There are friends who can respect one another's silence, and I see that gentle gardener going about his work in quietness while Jesus meditated and prayed apart; yet sometimes he would catch the look on Jesus' face, or a word falling from His lips, which was more to him than all his harvests. For any one to hear Jesus say Father in Gethsemane was worth a world's ransom. And to this man it may have been given to hear the mediatorial prayer St. John lost, and to preserve it for the Church. He doeth shrewd business who lendeth home or land to Christ, or best of all his heart, for it is the way of our Master to pay tribute not in silver or gold but in the spiritual treasures which last for ever. For-

The Sorrowful Way

tunate is that man who possesses the very ground on which a battle for freedom was fought, who has in his library the Bible which is stained with a martyr's blood, or the manuscript of Wordsworth's Ode on Immortality; but whose good fortune is to be compared with his to whom belonged Gethsemane, where the Lord endured His bitter Passion and gained unto Himself the victory?

Must we know him only as a certain young man? Is it impossible to call him by name, to discover him in other offices of friendship? Just over the summit of Olivet, and but a short distance from Gethsemane, was Bethany where Martha and Mary lived with their brother Lazarus. It was from their house Jesus went forth each morning in Passion Week till the last, to it He returned after the toil of the day. Was there no connection between the home of Bethany and the Garden of Gethsemane? Could Jesus have had two friends so devoted and so loving, living so near and so like one another as Mary's brother and this young man? Does not this faithful, retiring, mystical form, suggest the character of Lazarus? Over Lazarus hung the shadow of a terrible disease, for he was the son of Simon the leper, for him there could be no marriage or family joys. An only brother, he lived

The Sorrowful Way

with his sisters in that pathetic affection which is deepened by a common sorrow. Unto him had been vouchsafed an awful experience, since this man had lain four days under the power of death and then come back into the light of day and the affairs of human life. None love so intensely as those hidden and reserved natures, and one can understand that the heart of Lazarus was given to Jesus as the kindliest of dumb animals is devoted to its master. Each evening, as we suppose, he waited anxiously, going often to the brow of Olivet, till Jesus returned from Jerusalem, and his heart failed him when Jesus came not on

Passion Night. He lay down upon his bed but could not sleep; he arose and went where he expected the Master to be: so he was found clad in a linen garment, following Him whom he loved in the shadows of Gethsemane. For this fond soul was like unto the bride in the Song of Songs: " By night on my bed I sought him whom my soul loveth; I sought him, but I found him not. I will rise now and go about. . . . I will seek him whom my soul loveth."

Lazarus is the type of them whom God has called aside and made to walk in a solitary way; who are taken into secret places and see strange sights. With the

The Sorrowful Way

light-hearted gaiety of life and its practical methods of speech and action they can have no part, for life has been to them a sacred mystery. The ordinary forms of thought and the conventions of society cannot contain their experience, for what they know is beyond our present language and our prosaic rules. Like Dante they have been in hell; like St. Paul they have been in the third heaven; and they have heard things which it is not lawful to utter. They follow Jesus beneath the trees of Gethsemane, partakers of His love and travail. We, of the multitude, are startled by those separate souls and regard them with apprehension.

What is the meaning of this faraway look in their eyes, this awestruck accent in their speech, this preference of loneliness? Sometimes we grow irritable, and demand that they should declare themselves, who they are, what they are thinking, why they so carry themselves. We lay rough hands upon them, and would tear off the pure covering of their souls; whereupon they elude us and hide themselves in the protecting darkness of Gethsemane, where we know not the ways. It were wiser for us to respect their reserve and give no sign that they are seen. It is enough for us to carry the Lord with us in creeds and sacraments, along

The Sorrowful Way

the beaten road and where the light is shining; let us leave to them the darkness and the loneliness which are to such disciples as home. Nor let us boast, for if we hold the Master by many outward symbols they carry Him in their hearts, who, possessing Gethsemane, have also possessed Gethsemane's Lord.

The Bearer of Christ's Cross

The Bearer of Christ's Cross

WHEN a sudden remembrance of Christ's faithful love rises and overcomes our heart, we regard with wistful envy those disciples who rendered personal service to the Lord during the days of His humiliation. Joseph, who provided a home for Mary and the Holy Child; Mary, who discharged for His infancy the tenderest offices of love; the devoted women who ministered to Him of their substance; the owner of Gethsemane, who reserved to Jesus a quiet place where He might suffer and pray; the goodman who lent the Upper Room for the great Passover; Joseph of Arimathæa, who would not see Jesus laid in a malefactor's grave; the mourners who wrapt His body in spices and fair white linen — were one and all highly favoured, beside whom the great and mighty personages of that day are not to be mentioned. And yet one would rather have chosen to be Simon the Cyrenian, because he rendered unto Jesus a still more timely and intimate service.

They were, one and all, His true and kindly friends, who saw Him homeless and took Him in, who saw Him athirst and gave

The Sorrowful Way

Him drink, who saw Him neglected and honoured Him. They did well, and they did not miss their opportunity; they lightened Christ's load and comforted Christ's heart, but they did not stand in Christ's place. Had they withheld their hand His lot would have been harder, but He had still continued on His way. Once, however, the Lord was in such sore straits that His body failed Him and He was helpless. His mysterious agony in Gethsemane, His night-long trials, His cruel scourgings, His soul's sorrow had sapped for the time even His superb strength; and although He was willing to die upon the cross, it seemed likely that He would not be able to carry it to Calvary. Art, with her quick eye for a symbolic situation, has represented Him crushed unto the ground beneath the burden of the cross. It was at this moment a man came to His aid. When the two single beams are lifted from the Lord's bleeding shoulders and laid on the sturdy Cyrenian, Simon was not Jesus' servant nor His comforter. This man was what none other ever had been or ever would be in all the history of the Lord's Passion: he became for a brief space the substitute of Jesus.

Simon came that morning into Jerusalem *unconscious of the tragedy of life*. All the year this man, amid the labours and trials of ordinary life, had looked forward

The Sorrowful Way

and longed, like every loyal Jew, for the high Passover Feast. He came up with a goodly company along the ways of the Holy Land, and it might well be that the Cyrenian passed the place where Jesus had taken His disciples aside, and was telling them concerning His Passion. As a countryman Simon could not bear the crush and heat of the city, and, like unto the Master Himself, this Cyrenian was guest with friends in some neighbouring village. When Jesus went to the Garden of Gethsemane and wrestled in sore agony under the olive-trees, Simon lay down to rest and slept quietly. The morning light which saw Jesus dragged from palace to court with contumely and cruelty wakened Simon with its kindly rays, and the fresh, sweet air touched his face as with God's benediction. He left the simple home filled with Passover gladness, and took his way to the sacred city through the spring flowers and the singing of the birds. And as he travelled Simon lifted his head and rejoiced because the sun was shining in its glory on the Temple of God.

Are there not times when, like Simon the Cyrenian, we live at ease and reck not of the world's tragedy? We bid our household a good-morning as we meet after the darkness of the night has fled, and as the shadows begin to gather we bid one another a good-night —

The Sorrowful Way

the day beginning and closing for us in peace. God has been pleased to grant us health of body, success to labour, wealth of family love, and many priceless treasures of this life. Our faith is also quite untroubled, and as we look forward we see afar the city whose gates are one pearl, where is the Throne of God and of the Lamb. We do not despise, because we cannot even imagine the affliction of those who have been defeated and broken, who are lonely and bereaved, who look into black darkness and fear that God has forsaken them.

Simon became of a sudden *a witness of the tragedy of life* when he was caught in the crowd which accompanied Jesus to Calvary.

Companions of

Through the dense, struggling, excited mass of life the heavily-built countryman forced himself with insistent body till he came to the edge of the procession. First there were soldiers, and last there were soldiers. Soldiers beat back the human pressure on either side. Within the wall of mail two thieves carried their crosses to the place of execution, and after them followed another, also with His cross. It was His name which passed from lip to lip; it was this Man every one pressed to see. From his vantage Simon could peer in and get sight of Jesus — could catch the weariness of His face, and hear His panting breath as He trembled beneath the cross.

The Sorrowful Way

An irresistible curiosity seized him: he would see the end of this affair. Simon kept step with the soldiers, and from time to time he leant forward to look at Jesus. Did the contrast between the olive gardens, with their fretted sunlight, and the steaming, echoing streets, through which the Holiest was led in pain and shame, awaken this spectator's imagination? There, in his place outside, did he get a glimpse for an instant into the tears of things which lay so near to its joy on that spring day, when the fields were green and the birds were singing, and the Lord of them all was being tortured unto death?

What of ourselves, all bystanders in the Sorrowful Way? Does the veil drop from our eyes at a time, and is our heart melted within us, when, in the midst of business, as we hurry to and fro, a simple funeral passes with a few mourners, and reminds us that the bread-winner or the house-mother is gone? When on some great occasion the people keep holiday, with the sound of music and dancing, and we light upon a widow in her black? When in the public print one reads of some sickening outrage, whereby the light and honour of a family have been taken away, for whom there is now left no joy, no redress this side the grave? Everywhere, amid the bustle and gaiety of life, one is

The Sorrowful Way

touched by its underlying and far-reaching sorrow, as in a sweet country scene, where thinking of nothing but running water and spreading trees and wild roses and ripening corn, he comes of a sudden on a grave-yard, and entering, finds a newly-made grave with a young child's name on the stone.

Simon was forcibly *taken into the heart of the tragedy*. It was the merest accident, we should say, that he was selected; it might have been any other person in the crowd. They dare not lay hands on a great person to be Christ's cross-bearer, lest he should have them scourged for the insult. No priest in his high estate would condescend to touch the accursed tree with his finger-tips. For a Roman soldier it had been a loathsome degradation. The guard looked round, and they saw Simon. His prominence and his bulk, perhaps an unconscious sympathy growing on his face, attracted their eye. Here was a fellow nature had intended to be a carrier of loads, a common man who could make no complaint, a simpleton who had pity on an outcast. So it came to pass that, without more ado, and before Simon knew what had happened, he was dragged out from among the people, and the cross was on his shoulders, and he was walking beside Jesus to Calvary. Oh, good fortune of the Cyrenian to have a stout body and to be

The Sorrowful Way

born a countryman and to carry a kindly heart, for it has won him an honour denied to kings and conquerors.

Some day it may happen that, having made his visit to our neighbours, Death will have a mind to call on us, and we shall go softly about our changed house in sad amazement. Or a fleecy cloud, which only lent a pleasing softness to the arch of blue, will suddenly gather into a thunder-cloud and lay desolate our golden cornfields, and our prosperity will be no more. Or a fine passage from the Prophets, whose literary grace and felicitous imagery we have often tasted, will fling aside its embroidered cloak and spring upon us, gripping our conscience and heart with iron hand. We shall be taken from the midst of the multitude, among which we were hidden, and the cross we had seen on others' shoulders shall rest on our own. Before, we had marched along on the outskirts of life; now, we are brought into its secret place, where Jesus travelleth with His companions along the Sorrowful Way to fulfil the Will of God.

In the heart of the tragedy Simon met with Jesus. Many persons had interviews with Jesus, but none was so favoured as this Cyrenian, for they journeyed together within an iron wall. No

The Sorrowful Way

man could interrupt or annoy, neither priest nor people; they were so close together that the cross would seem to be upon them both, and would gain them the immunity of the dying — who are left alone. What Jesus said to His substitute in the passage to Calvary, Simon never told, and if he had, then ought the cross to have been laid once more on him, with no Jesus by his side. That Jesus spoke to him as He did to few in all His ministry there can be no doubt, since no one could render Jesus the least service without being instantly repaid, and this man succoured Him in His dire extremity. When a single woman repaired the neglect of Simon the Pharisee, the Lord must needs send her into peace. If a Samaritan drew Him water from the well in the heat of the day, He gave her to drink of the water of life. Let Mary of Bethany anticipate the crown of thorns with her spikenard, and the Master ordered that this deed be told wherever the Gospel went. Does some one pluck out the thorns, and bind a napkin tenderly round the wounded head? Behold the Lord cannot leave the tomb without folding up that napkin and laying it in a place by itself, in token of His gratitude. With what kindness He must have spoken to His cross-

The Sorrowful Way

bearer as they went together to Calvary under one cross and common disgrace! For a short while this man carried the load of wood, and in return Jesus carried his sin and that of his children after him; for by the time this Gospel was given unto the world Simon is known as the head of a distinguished Christian house, a man honoured in his sons, the father of Alexander and Rufus. Within the iron bands of affliction, and alone with the Redeemer, one learns more secrets and gathers richer treasures than in a lifetime of ease and gaiety. When Simon came that morning to Jerusalem there was no cross on Mount Calvary, and when

The Sorrowful Way

he returned to his country home in the evening there was no cross again. Nothing of the great tragedy could be seen save the trampled grass and a drop or two of blood; but in the meanwhile Jesus had accomplished the deliverance of the world, and Simon the Cyrenian had carried the Lord's cross.

A Noble Lady

A Noble Lady

IT is characteristic of the Gospels to describe at length, and with wealth of detail, the effect of Jesus on the "common people" till we see the multitude crowding the lake shore to hear Him, sitting in companies on the grass, pressing into private houses, filling the temple courts; a flowing, buoyant tide of life. They are amazed, enthusiastic, perplexed, furious before our eyes. There they are so carried with admiration that they would fain make Jesus a king; here they are so swayed by national prejudice that they send Him to the cross; while a few choice souls separate themselves from the mass to follow Him for ever. One then bethinks himself of those who are not seen in public places and do not stand in crowds, who maintain a studied reserve, and will not parade their feelings. Did the class who are not weary nor heavy-laden, who are cushioned round with ease and live in sheltered places, ever hear of Jesus, and what did they think of Him? Humble women, after the fashion of Mary of Bethany and her sister Martha, captivated by His spiritual attractions, gave Him welcome not only in their cottages

The Sorrowful Way

but also in their hearts. Did the great ladies of the day, to whom spikenard was a common thing, do homage to the Lord?

Whatever may have been the case in that age, there has been no other since in which Jesus as He passed on His way has not called women forth from every circumstance of rank and luxury to carry His hard cross. They were not all slaves and working women who died in the Roman persecutions, for if Blandina was a slave girl, Perpetua was a patrician. St. Theresa, the type of mystical passion, was a noble's daughter, and St. Elizabeth of Hungary, who gave herself to works of charity and the nursing of loathsome diseases, was a queen. French women of high rank sheltered the Huguenot pastors in their straits, and Samuel Rutherford from his prison writes to the wives of Scots lords who had taken the covenant. Last century, Lady Huntingdon devoted herself and her substance to the revival of religion in England; and in the middle of this century, the Duchess of Gordon gave herself to the same work in Scotland. The voice of Jesus has penetrated into castles, and His attraction has overcome the pride of seclusion and the power of this present world. When the Sorrowful Way lay at their door, delicate and fastidious women

The Sorrowful Way

have arisen and passed into it, that they might follow Christ.

His own age was no exception, nor has He done more by His Evangel than by His Presence, for He did touch the only high society of His land. It was the misfortune of Galilee to have for its tetrarch Herod Antipas, to whom religion was a superstition and virtue an offence. Could there be any more unlikely place for Jesus' word than in that decadent circle, where a dancing-girl won a prophet's head for her reward and a wanton ruled the king? Jesus had certainly no speech with Herod himself, although He sent him the one contemptuous word which passed

His lips, and He was once asked to perform miracles to please Herod and his courtiers, as if He had been some common magician. While that miserable court was flaunting its moral disgrace in the face of the Jewish world, a handful of godly women, amid many hindrances doubtless and much scorn, counted it an honour to support Jesus in His prophetical work, of whom one name has been preserved — Joanna, the wife of Chusa, Herod's steward.

One circle in the land was still more exclusive, to which Jesus could have no direct access. Like the English in India, the Romans lived apart from the Jews — divided in blood, in religion, in

The Sorrowful Way

pride — conquerors among the conquered. There seems, on first sight, no common ground where this Prophet and a Roman could meet. If some official heard of Jesus as he dealt with public affairs there was little to catch his attention. Jesus would only be to him as an Indian fakir of local sanctity to an English magistrate. As for the Roman's wife, in her proud isolation one would not expect her ever to hear His name or know that Jesus lived. How persuasive, therefore, must have been our Master's teaching, how convincing His character, how mysterious His influence, that Jesus was known in the palace of the Roman procurator, and had won for His friend Procula, Pilate's wife.

It is true that the mysterious attraction of the Jews had caught the jaded imagination of the grand Roman ladies, and it may be that Procula was a proselyte, but in the circumstances of fierce hostility between her husband and the Jews it was not likely. One rather imagines that in the weariness of her exile she had given ear to the talk of a Jewish maid, and that from the midst of petty gossip the story of Jesus had emerged and caught Procula's ear. His sudden appearance in Jewish life, His gracious words, His marvellous works, His winsome personality, His tender compassion, appealed

The Sorrowful Way

to her womanly nature. The hardship of His lot, the unselfishness of His aims, the opposition of the Pharisees, the schemes of the priests, the dangers which encompassed Him, completed the attraction. From a single incident or even a dozen words a sympathetic and sensitive person can estimate and approve a character. Whether her informant understood the situation or not it was clear as day to Procula. It was one of the repeated tragedies of life, a gentle soul full of spiritual visions and beautiful deeds, hated and persecuted by bigotry and fanaticism. Curiosity passed into interest and ended in devotion, till she hungered for news of

Jesus, and devoured greedily His every word or deed. Between Jesus and Procula there grew up a mystical friendship which was quite independent of sight, and has been repeated in all the ages, whenever a fine nature discovers in the Master the perfection it has ever sought, and is satisfied. As the plot thickened round the Lord, and His enemies waxed in rage, this secret friend shared the Lord's Passion, till on the night of His betrayal, when He was dragged through Jerusalem, she was with Him in her dreams. While apostles slept her heart kept watch, and in the early morning light when Jesus stood before the Roman judge, with

The Sorrowful Way

none of all whom He had helped to say one word for Him, Procula, with the vision of the night still upon her soul, sent a message to her husband and interceded that he should do no harm to a righteous man.

One has no sooner realised the character of Procula than he must have a profound sympathy with Pilate's wife, and a keen imagination of her history. What scheming, heartless mother sold such a daughter to this selfish, worthless noble? What a disillusionment and profanation of the most sacred mystery of life for this woman to find herself united to a man she could not honour nor respect. What agonies of shame and con-

Companions of

tempt must have been Procula's lot as the character of her husband opened up before her eyes — his watchful self-regard, his scheming ambition, his calculated cruelty, his cowardly cunning. When a woman of noble temper is called to this experience, she tastes the very dregs of humiliation, and carries the heaviest cross that can be laid on a woman's soul. As the daughters of Jerusalem, their faces aged with care and their hands worn with labour, saw Pilate's wife carried past in her litter, the flash of the gems on her white hands, and the pride of her patrician face, they would envy Procula in her luxury and high estate, and could never guess

The Sorrowful Way

that she would have exchanged with the poorest woman wedded to an honest man.

The woman, whose lot one pities most, is not the lonely heart which has missed the prize of life, nor the trustful one who has been betrayed, nor the victim whose sufferings are known to all, nor the drudge whose life is beaten down by toil. They have their burden, but it is in each case lighter than hers whose soul is proud, and whose husband maintains her in material comfort and serves her with fair words, who may even after a fashion respect and love her, but who is utterly selfish and unprincipled. Other women of lower rank and coarser nature may ventilate their grievance and find relief. Unto this woman it is not allowed to complain or expose her sorrow: her traditions and pride compel her to silence and concealment. Perhaps the bravest sufferer in the world is a pure and delicate woman who is gay and smiles with a shamed and tortured heart.

Unto Procula was given a noble service to stand in the shadow and to be her husband's saviour. No one, until the end of all things, will ever know what men have owed unto women of spiritual instincts and faithful hearts. The man has played his part in the open amid the public praise or blame, and few guess how he was

The Sorrowful Way

either inspired or restrained by a woman. Behind St. John was his mother Salome, behind Pilate was his wife Procula. We know what good one man did; we do not know who moved him. We know what evil another man did; we do not know what evil a woman hindered. But we do know that in the great event and moral crisis of Pilate's life Procula pleaded for righteousness and Christ and almost had her way.

Procula failed that day before the force of circumstances and Pilate's lean heart, and it doubtless seemed to her as if her cup of mortification were full when her husband and a Roman Governor sent Jesus of Nazareth to the cross. The guilt was hers, too, for she was his wife, and she would share the punishment which was sure to come. She accepted her lot, and when Pilate reaped what he had sown Procula went into exile with him. As she had been his best adviser in the days of his power, so this gentle and honourable woman would be his one comforter in the days of his adversity. It pleases one to believe that the evangelist of Pilate's home spake not in vain at last, and that Jesus' prayer for His murderers covered Pontius Pilate. One day the trial of that spring morning in Jerusalem will be repeated, with a certain transposition of judge and prisoner. Then Pilate was

The Sorrowful Way

on the judgment seat and Jesus was at the bar; now Christ is on the throne of His glory and Pilate awaits sentence. Procula alone of the three has the same honourable place. Once she interceded with her husband for Jesus when His people called for His death and His friends were silent through fear. Again she pleads, but now it is for her repentant husband, and it is with Him who has all power in heaven and earth; and though she failed with Pilate for Jesus she will surely succeed with Christ for Pilate, and unto her, as to many another lifelong martyr, will be given for a recompense of reward her husband's soul.

The Daughters of Jerusalem

The Daughters of Jerusalem

ONE of the most powerful works of realistic art is Christ before Pilate, and Munkacsy has brought out with much felicity, that of all persons present, only two had any sympathy with the Master. Pontius Pilate on his judgment-seat is calculating with his fingers, as if it were a sum of arithmetic, the chances of action, — whether it would be expedient to acquit or condemn the prisoner. Two aged students of the law are discussing a fine point

— whether, say, the Messiah could come out of Nazareth, or whether He would work miracles on the Sabbath. An elder of the people, increased in goods and swollen with pride, leans back in his seat and eyes Jesus with contempt, appraising at its money value His simple garment. One scribe, more thoughtful and candid than his fellows, is not certain about the situation, and is asking himself whether this man be really a blasphemer as they had concluded, or a prophet in disguise. An orator of powerful presence and brazen countenance, a typical demagogue, has struck an attitude, demanding the condemnation of the accused. The crowd beyond

The Sorrowful Way

is surging to and fro, a mass of senseless, fanatical faces, and one young man, shutting his eyes and opening his mouth, after the fashion of his kind in all ages, is bawling, "Crucify Him! crucify Him!" A Roman soldier, detached, indifferent, dominant, keeps back the rabble with the butt of his spear, and protects Jesus from unlicensed violence. Neither among rulers nor mob neither in judge nor soldier has the prisoner a friend.

And yet even in this evil and hostile atmosphere there are two people whose faces have no hatred, whose faces pity Jesus. Beside the wall and behind the seat of the scribes a woman is standing with her child in her arms. She is a young mother with a serene, comely face, and she is a daughter of the people. Drawn by an irresistible interest, she had risen early and fought her way into Pilate's Judgment Hall, carrying the little one with her, as a working mother must when she goes abroad. She had secured a place whence the face of Jesus could be seen, and she held her boy that he might share the sight. Sorrow and concern, respect and affection mingle on her countenance; for her judge and elders, people and soldiers have disappeared; she sees Jesus only, bound and helpless. Was there between this woman and Jesus some personal

The Sorrowful Way

tie, such as the last three years had woven between many and the Master? Had He healed her boy sick unto death and given him back unto his mother? Was this one of the mothers who brought their children unto Jesus, this a child on whose head Jesus' unbound hands had rested? Did she carry in her own experience the proof of His goodness, against which all charges of priests and Pharisees were vain?

It needeth not there should have been any incident: it is enough that she was a woman with her child. Among all classes of the community save one Jesus had friends and foes. If a Roman official condemned Him a Roman officer showed greater faith in Him than any one in Israel; if the Pharisees hounded Jesus to death two of their number gave Him honourable burial; if the mob of Jerusalem were bitter against Him, the Galileans were hot in His favour. One class only was undivided because they were unanimous in their love of Jesus — the women with the little children. They did not suspect or question, or spy upon Him: they trusted, served, adored Him. Women made ready their sons to be His disciples, afforded a home to Him in His weariness, supported Him with their substance, anointed Him for burial, wrapt His Body in spices. They never

The Sorrowful Way

vexed His heart, never disappointed Him, never failed Him; they sustained Him by their sympathy all His ministry, and they paid Him their last public tribute of devotion on the Sorrowful Way.

It was surely almost incredible, and altogether horrible, that after Jesus had lived three years among them after the very likeness of God, in grace and compassion, the whole nation — priests, scholars, merchants, working folk — should unite in one fierce confederacy of hate, and cry aloud like wild beasts for His crucifixion, and follow Him to the Cross with satisfaction, and relent not till He was dead. And chiefly it was saddest that the

Companions of

working folk, from whom He sprang, whom He loved, whom He helped, should have been hottest against Him; and it is enough to make their friends despair of the ungrateful, fickle, foolish people. Yet is it never to be forgotten that one half only of the people were mad and wicked, and that the other half were full of insight and wisdom. If the men, misled by priests and bigots, rent the sky with their yells, "Crucify Him! crucify Him!" their wives, sisters, and daughters had a tender heart to Jesus, and followed Him as He carried His Cross along the Sorrowful Way with weeping and lamentations.

It is not unknown that men

The Sorrowful Way

should criticise women as persons deficient in judgment and unacquainted with affairs, while they congratulate themselves because they are shrewd and capable. This comparison is doubtless just on that lower level where we deal with rules and plans and words and the machinery of life. When we rise to the tableland of Goodness and Truth, then men move slowly with the heavy foot of reason, but women fly swiftly with the wings of instinct. Very likely it could be shown unto the satisfaction of cold-blooded men, with fixed ideas and traditional prejudices, that Jesus was a heretic and a dangerous teacher; that it might be safer for the Jewish faith and commonwealth that He be removed and silenced. One imagines that in debate the husband would have the better of his wife, backed as he was by the judgment of the wise and great men of the nation, and that his wife would take refuge in a woman's last fortress — her inward conviction. "There are the facts," he would say, with coarse masculine common sense; and "I know," she would reply, with the certainty of an instinct. Time is the final arbiter, and time has decided in favour of the womanly instinct: the mighty ecclesiastics and shrewd men of the world were wrong, and committed the master crime of history; simple working women

The Sorrowful Way

were right, and did their best to redeem the crime. When the daughters of Jerusalem wept over Jesus they made atonement for the rulers of the nation.

Their tears fell on the heart of Jesus as a healing balm — His friends were faithful to the last; their cries broke His silence — He must render them a last service. They had pitied Him in His Passion and He was grateful to the honest hearts: in their womanly self-sacrifice they had given Him what they rather needed for themselves. He was carrying the Cross for a brief space: they were bowed down beneath the load of labour all their days. He was silenced and

Companions of

tortured for a day: they had no appeal from oppression till they died. He exhausted His own suffering: they suffered once in themselves, once in their children. As they looked on Him, the marks of unspeakable insult on His face, the blood stains on His white garment, the body yielding beneath the Cross, there seemed no sorrow like unto His. As He looked on them, their care-worn faces, on whom the burden of the family had fallen, their youth aged before its time, their hands hardened with drudgery; as He thought of the narrowness, sameness, toilsomeness, weariness of their lot, it seemed to Jesus that there was no sorrow like unto theirs. He spake

The Sorrowful Way

unto the generations which were to come; He looked beyond the calamity which must befal this fanatical city; He accepted the working women of the race of all ages as His fellow sufferers in a longer travail. "Weep not for Me, My Passion is brief; weep for yourselves and for your children, yours is continual."

Martyrdom has its kinds and degrees, and the honourable word has been too much restricted and localised. If any one be burned or tortured, if any one suffer cruel slander or insult, if any one deny himself innocent joy and just ease for the sake of faith, then doubtless he belongs to the "noble army." If one simply lives not for himself but for others from childhood to old age, without relief, without joy, without outlook, then that person in his obscure, commonplace, endless travail, is surely of the same blood and has won the same honour. This is the life of a woman of the class which labours and is heavy-laden, in every age and in every land. While still a child she is withdrawn from play and baptised into the drudgery of the little household, gaining a pathetic knowledge before her time. Before she has come to womanhood the girl is sent to service, where she has no leisure, no rights of individuality, no gaiety of youth. Her

The Sorrowful Way

idyll of love, when it comes, is fettered by circumstances and shorn of romance. With her marriage her last hour of rest has gone, and before her now lies the travail of birth, the anxious charge of children, the waiting on her husband, the careful management of small affairs. She is the first to rise and the last to sleep, and between the rising up and the lying down there is only toil which knows no remission, which descends to the humblest offices. What doth this patient, selfless woman also endure at the hands of a brutal husband, by the disrespect of rough children, through the squalor of circumstances. For her there remaineth no rest till some day they fold the thin worn hands on her breast and let the tired house-mother here have her long sleep.

Yet if the daughters of Jerusalem miss their rest they have even here their reward. Beyond any other class in the community, save, perhaps, physicians they enter into the very secret of the religion of Jesus and receive the impress of His character. They need not to be reminded of His Cross for it is ever on their shoulders; they have not to be summoned to self-denial for it is their daily unconscious life. Amid the limitations and hardships of their lot they exhibit the meekness, endurance, charity, mercy of Jesus.

The Sorrowful Way

They realise the parable of the Good Samaritan, and fulfil the Law of Love. This is the truth in the legend of Veronica, which is the poem of the Daughters of Jerusalem. A woman, full of pity for Jesus as He fell to the ground beneath the cross, stooped and wiped the bloody sweat from His face. When she recovered her handkerchief there was no stain upon it, but instead thereof the very likeness of the Lord.

A Malefactor

A Malefactor

WHEN Jesus was crucified between two thieves, His enemies had inflicted their last indignity, and the irony of history was complete. From the beginning of His public life unto the end, whatever He had deserved was refused Him, and whatever He had not deserved was rendered unto Him. Beyond all the prophets who had ever taught the nation Jesus revealed the Father, and He was judged guilty of blasphemy. There was no worthy rite of the Jewish religion He did not observe, and the anointed priests of God demanded His death. In His discourses He expounded the law of Moses most perfectly, and its guardians dogged His steps with spies. For the sake of the people and their neglected souls He refused to come to terms with the rulers, and the blinded people vociferously demanded His crucifixion. Above all others He had loved and blessed the helpless classes of the community — women and children — and they, poor souls, had to witness His agony. Against the Romans He was careful to say no word, and a Roman played the coward and betrayed Roman justice that Jesus might not escape.

The Sorrowful Way

He was the holiest man ever seen in Israel or on the face of the earth, and the Church did not rest night or day till Jesus was crucified between two thieves, after a brigand had been preferred before Him. The moral laws of the universe were inverted for three years in the case of this man, so that while Herod was king and Pilate was governor and Caiaphas high priest, Jesus was sent to the cross.

Standing in that day one could only have seen a ghastly injustice; standing at this distance one finds in this last humiliation a proof of Jesus' utter sympathy with His brethren and another chapter in His redemption. Before He had associated freely with simple folk who knew no theology, with Samaritans who were heretics, with publicans who were political offenders, with women who were social outcasts, but He had not yet touched the lowest depths of human life. Such people had wandered without a shepherd, they had fallen into error, they had become the slaves of circumstances, they had played the fool before man and God; but they were not criminals, and had not upon their lives the most hopeless and indelible brand. Without the association of the three crosses one had not been able to say of our Master that He has condescended to the last identification with our race. As He

The Sorrowful Way

dies between two thieves, stretching out His arms towards them, and inclining His ear unto their cry, He embraceth all men within His Evangel and within His heart.

Jesus' conversation with the thief who repented is indeed a Gospel in brief, very full and comforting, wherein many mysteries of the spiritual life are revealed. *When a man comes to his lowest estate, he will find Jesus beside him.* Sometimes a false glory of romance is cast round a criminal so that he becometh as a hero unto the foolish people who are ever inclined to be led astray by marsh lights, born of corruption, and to belittle the shining of the sun. So it came to pass that a brigand took such hold on the perverted imagination of Jerusalem that the multitude preferred Barabbas to the Lord of Glory, and in their admiration the miserable man had an antidote to his sense of guilt, so that what was surely the very moment of degradation for our race was his crowning honour. But the thief of the cross was not a chief in the profession of crime; he was only a common and ordinary evil-doer whose petty offences were redeemed by no audacity and made no appeal. His would be a common-place history. A foolish child who would receive no instruction, a headstrong lad who would not be controlled, an idle

The Sorrowful Way

young man who would not work, he had drifted into evil company. He had committed some misdemeanour and been once forgiven; he had repeated it and been punished; he had turned again to his foolishness and had been cast finally out of respectability; he had been at last caught and condemned to death. What else could be done with him, this piece of worthless human refuse? What loss could there be to the community by his death? — there would be a gain. Who would miss him? None — his mother being dead. Within an hour or two this obscure and abject wretch would be blotted out from the earth, and so would end a squalid tragedy.

Companions of

There was indeed but one man living to whom this dying outcast was dear, and it had come to pass that the two were hanging side by side in a common disgrace and rejection. Almost certainly this thief had heard of Jesus in the talk of the roadside; very likely he had hung on the outskirts of the crowd when Jesus preached, and words of the Lord had floated out to him such as, "Come unto Me, ye that labour and are heavy laden, and I will give you rest." As he was after all a man, this abject must have had his own regrets and dreams; he must have wished he had done something with his morsel of life, and had not flung it into the ditch. It was then his

The Sorrowful Way

opportunity to repent and begin again: in the Friend of sinners was hope, and a welcome for his kind. If such a thought visited his mind he was hindered by his pride, which had not yet been finally vanquished, and by the distance of Jesus, who was then in a high place. Both barriers had been broken down, for he was now fastened to a cross, beaten and despairing, and Jesus had been cast forth by the people as one not worthy to live. They met, this poor wreck of a man and Jesus, the Saviour of all men, flung together by the will of God, each on his cross.

When a man is hardened by the punishment of law, he may be soft-

ened by the sight of goodness. It was no doubt right and needful that this malefactor be condemned by public opinion, and driven out from the midst of law-abiding people, and laid under various pains, and it might be to the gain of society that he cease to live. By such severity a community protects itself from evil-doers, and places a premium on virtue, but it is not by such measures that the soul of the sinner is saved. As one penalty was added to another upon this life, the soul within also added one sin to another, growing not in penitence, obedience, well-doing, but in bitterness, lawlessness, violence, till this enemy of society came to such

The Sorrowful Way

a height of hatred that he joined with his fellow in cursing Christ.

This was the bitter fling of moral despair, not the voice of his better self, and as he hung beside the Lord a change came over the malefactor. He knew little of Jesus, but he was certain that Jesus had not deserved to suffer. He knew little of himself, but he was certain that he had deserved to suffer. The sinless hung upon one tree, the sinner on another, and the grace of the Lord, who prayed for His enemies, and endured in silence, began to tell on his soul. In the presence of this august purity, of this tender pity, the malefactor examined his life and judged his sins. What the law with all its penalties could not accomplish, Jesus wrought, who neither threatened nor reproached, who only prayed and suffered. Upon His Cross Jesus was stronger than all the officers of justice, for they could only pierce the malefactor's body, but He had pierced his soul.

When a man maketh a prayer to Jesus it is best to leave himself altogether in Jesus' hands. It was given unto this malefactor in his low estate to attain unto a triumphant faith and to render a grateful honour unto Jesus. When his friends had forsaken the Lord, this man became His disciple; when his nation had condemned

The Sorrowful Way

the Lord, this man justified Him; when the Romans sent Him to a cross, this man acknowledged Him as King of heaven and earth. Considering all things, this was the highest faith in the Gospels, which believed in spite of sight; and, considering all things, this was the finest tribute paid to Jesus in the Gospels, which of a sudden transformed a cross into a throne. And the very essence of this faith and honour lay in the utter self-abandonment of the prayer. There were many things the malefactor did not need, but might have asked; many things he needed, and could have asked; many things he needed, and did not know how to ask. His case was extreme, his time was short, his opportunity immense. His wisdom and humility were also great. He cast himself on the Lord's goodwill and wisdom, and on the riches of His liberality. "One thing alone I crave in the day of Thy power: give one thought to him who hung beside Thee on his cross, and it sufficeth." And doubtless one thought of the Lord is salvation for us as for this malefactor.

When Jesus dealeth with a man He useth such knowledge as a man has. Long ago this man's mother had given him lessons in religion and had taught him concerning Paradise; how, as the race had gone out from a garden,

The Sorrowful Way

to a garden would God's chosen people return, and there live in peace and joy. She would teach him God's commandments and beseech him to keep them that he might see long life, and they might meet in the Paradise of God. With such instructions and hopes would the mother of this man train her boy, and bind them on his heart with love. As seed would she drop her words into his mind, and water them with prayer, rejoicing at the appearance of the green herb, when her lad in his best moments responded to her love and promised obedience. Afterwards came the flood, which devastated the spring pastures and covered them with blackness. If that mother were living on earth, where we see but do not foresee, when he played the fool, her faith would be sorely tried and when she died in sorrow the neighbours would be apt to consider that her labours had been in vain, and that the good had been finally destroyed. It really only waited the light of Christ to awake and spring again. Did not the remembrance of early days awake in the malefactor's breast at the sight of Jesus, and when he spake of the Messiah's kingdom was it not his mother's teaching? Above the waste of sin rose at last the tender grass of repentance and faith, and, as we

The Sorrowful Way

imagine, the fond labour of a mother was repaid when the malefactor returned to God.

When Jesus saveth a man, His grace is independent of time. For this man was in a day converted from his sin and perfected in holiness, so that within a few hours he was in hell, where he cursed the Lord, and in heaven, where he stood with Jesus in Paradise. Unto the faith which could recognise the Lord in the dust of death and believe in a kingdom for Him who was dying on a cross, all things were possible. It also became the Lord to signalise His victory over sin by a magnificent achievement, and by one sweep of His arm to lift a sinner from the lowest depths to the heights of glory. It is told in an excellent legend of the early Church how the penitent malefactor, relying on the Lord's word, took his way to the gate of Paradise and sought entrance, and how the holy angels assured him that whatsoever the Lord had said would be performed, but that he must wait till Jesus had returned from the lower places, whither He had gone to release the blessed Dead. So the malefactor stood by the gate while the angels held converse with him regarding Calvary, and Heaven bent over to see the firstfruits of the Lord's redemption. Then came the Lord with His company of patriarchs, prophets, martyrs,

The Sorrowful Way

from our forefather Adam to John the Baptist, and as they passed all looked at him, for this malefactor was the beginning of the New Testament Church. But I dare to think that, although the Lord smiled on him and all the saints bade him welcome, this man waited till he saw his mother, and they went together into Paradise.

A Roman Officer

A Roman Officer

IT is not to be taken for granted that he was a better man than his fellow officers in the garrison of Jerusalem, but it may be assumed that he did not relish his day's work. When a soldier is called to war or wounds he is proud, for this is the height of his calling; when he is detached to guard an execution he is filled with disgust, for this is a humiliation. With his company this centurion had gone on duty in the morning at

Pilate's Palace, and it was late afternoon before they were released. He had heard the trial of Jesus and the howling of the rabble: he had handed Jesus over to his men for scourging, and looked on with a callousness born of a rough life: he had escorted Jesus and the malefactors through the streets, and taken care that they were kept safe for the legal punishment: he had selected the site for the crosses and overseen from a height the nailing of the condemned: when the crosses were raised with their quivering load he satisfied himself that they were firmly set, and then through the long hours, as the priests

The Sorrowful Way

mocked and his men gambled for the garments, and the crucified suffered, he sat on his horse, silent, watchful, immovable. When the criminals were proved to be dead and the bodies had been disposed of, and the crosses removed, he gathered his company together and marched them back to their barracks. He went to his room; his servant removed the heavy armour which had been as a fiery prison in the scorching sunlight, and brought his master a cup of wine. It had been a long day for the centurion, and a sorry day's work, and he was glad in his soul that it was over.

Yet as the shadows gathered

in his room and he sat by himself, he knew that this spring day would never pass from his memory. Very likely he had assisted at many crucifixions, and might have to assist at many more before he was recalled from this land of trouble, but he had never met any prisoner like Jesus. As this Man stood in His whiteness before Pilate, He was distinguished and placed apart by a certain dignity of manhood and bravery of soul which neither bonds nor insults could obscure, which they only threw into relief. Ordinary men had been degraded by the scourging and the mocking: this Man left the degradation with

The Sorrowful Way

His enemies. Common men had cried out in their pain as they were fastened to the wood: this Man lifted up His voice in supplication. As unhappy wretches hung upon their crosses they rent the air with oaths, but this Man cared for the mother who wept at the foot of the cross. Once He did lift up His voice in sore agony, but it was the mysterious sorrow of the soul, not any pain of the body which affected Him. His last cry was not one of defeat, but of triumph, as of one who had given him a great task and had completed it. Upon the blunt and honest soldier this spectacle of moral heroism had its due effect, and it needed not the darkness and the earthquake to call forth his confession "This Man was a son of God."

It were untrue to read into this utterance the meaning of the creeds, for the centurion was certainly not a Christian theologian, nor were it profitable for this were to lose the value of his testimony. One must exercise imagination and reconstruct the circumstances. As a pagan this man had his theology and believed in beings of another world — stronger, braver, wiser than ourselves, — who on occasion appeared and took part in the affairs of this life. As a man he had his ideal of manhood, how one

The Sorrowful Way

ought to carry himself in the battle, and he had seen many whom he had approved, good comrades, fearless soldiers, loyal Romans. This day one had surpassed them all, since to an unshaken fortitude in the sorest trial he had added a singular sweetness and equanimity of soul. Nothing in the way of manliness so strong, so modest, so winning, had the centurion ever witnessed, and he could not believe that any other had ever beheld the like. The Jews might call this man a false prophet and a blasphemer, it was to be expected of their ill-temper and blind fanaticism. If he knew anything at all of the world and of men this

Jesus was lifted above Jews and Romans alike: He was nothing less than "a Son of God."

The excellency of our Master cometh not after the same fashion to every one's soul, but hath various avenues of access. Some have been arrested by the insight and authority of His words, and have been convinced that He is a teacher sent from God. They are clever people, and have received Jesus by the intellect. Some have been charmed by the perfect grace of Jesus' character, and have seen in Him the very love of God. They are emotional people, and have received Jesus by the heart. There are others to whom the Lord has come as the revelation

The Sorrowful Way

and incarnation of duty; as one who has kept the eternal law without rebate; as one who has made righteous living visible and glorious. They are practical people and they accept the Master with their conscience. For years they have been doing their duty with the best light they had, and in the best way they could, without boasting, and with many lights. They have also an unexpressed and unrealised idea of how things ought to be done, and this secret standard keeps them humble. One day they behold it fulfilled in the Master, and nothing will persuade them afterwards that Jesus is as one of ourselves.

It is certain that we are apt to

do less than justice to this class, who are chiefly men, and of whom this officer remains an excellent type. They have neither mind nor relish for the august mysteries of religion, its problems, theories, doctrines; and openly declare themselves ignorant or weary of such great matters. They are therefore judged to be unbelieving and unspiritual. Or they are insensible to the chief experiences of the religious life. They neither weep nor sing as others do with joyful fervour, and are ever suspicious of these high emotions. They are therefore counted cold and worldly. Yet is it to be remembered that one may revel in a creed and have no share in the Christ life;

The Sorrowful Way

that one may overflow with sentiment and neglect Christ's commandments. Those whom we mean would not call themselves religious at all, and have a very lowly idea of their place before God and man; and yet, without doctrine or experience, they have come to the heart of religion, because they are keeping a good conscience and fulfilling the Will of God.

What a multitude of men can be found in every land whose one idea is not to save their souls, or to earn a reward, but simply to do the work God has laid to their hand — to make provision for those whom they love, or who are left to their charge; to help any unfortunate person in trouble; to serve the commonwealth in some lowly place. They are diligent and honourable merchants, workmen putting their last grain of skill into the task, sailors standing by the ship through the wildest seas, shepherds saving the sheep in the winter's storm, servants faithful in the least things to the family under whose roof they have lived. Upon their conscientious and unremitting labour depends the welfare of society, and they do their work hardly and sorely. Theirs oftentimes is loss, disappointment, pain, danger, and yet they make no moan, no parade. Theirs is sometimes irksome and hateful work, but do it they will

The Sorrowful Way

till it be finished, without asking any credit or applause. Under the blazing sun they keep guard, and in the evening, when they are released, neither they nor any one else says or thinks that these modest, faithful men have done well.

Among all the companions of the "Sorrowful Way" the centurion has the humblest place, and it may seem bold to associate him with Jesus. He was not like unto the apostles, nor the godly women, nor the private friends of Jesus, nor even as the penitent malefactor. He met Jesus for the first time on the Way, and nothing passed between him and the Master save the stroke of the nails. Jesus had

The Sorrowful Way

yielded up the ghost before the centurion made his confession, and that honest man never expected to hear of it again, as his kind would be much astonished to learn that they had done any good thing; but when next he saw the Lord, Jesus had not forgotten, and unto this nameless Roman officer that word would be fulfilled, " If any man confess Me before men, him will I confess before My Father and the holy angels."

The Funeral
Of Jesus

The Funeral
Of Jesus

TWO spectacles are common to every class, and have affected the mind in every age. The one is the public celebration of joy — a wedding; the other of sorrow — a funeral; both are the witness of love. At their approach they arrest instant attention, and cast their spell on the most callous people. Pure hearts wish happiness to the bride in her whiteness, whether she be princess or peasant; kindly hearts pray God's consolations for the mourners in their black, whether it be Darby following Joan to her rest, or young children weeping for their lost mother. He is altogether heartless who is not gladdened or solemnised by these mysteries of human life, brought before one as in a sacrament. They represent the poles of feeling, yet they are not equal in power, for the sacrament of lamentation has an altogether peculiar majesty. Should the two processions meet at the gate of the churchyard, whither we all come in our chief moments, it is the children of joy who yield to the children of sorrow. Before the signs of loss and woe gladness bows her head and departs; the poorest funeral

The Sorrowful Way

is invested with the awful and omnipotent authority of death.

Among all the funerals ever seen on the earth surely the most pathetic was that of Jesus. His very body, tortured and pierced, belonged not to His mother and His friends, but to His enemies, and He had not, what the humblest Galilean would have, a place of burial. Having bought the souls of men from the power of the enemy with His own precious blood, His earthly Body had to be redeemed, as we guess, with silver and gold, from a Roman magistrate; and having opened the Kingdom of Heaven to all believers with His pierced hand, a rich man had to afford Him the hospitality of a tomb. What a sad irony it was to take down His Body from the Cross. How helpless it lay in their hands, with the double weight of death, which once was so charged with life that if one only touched the hem of its encircling garment she had healing of her long disease. Very tenderly they closed His eyes, which had beheld every honest man with love, and had wept over Jerusalem, to whose welcome the children had leaped from their mother's arms, before whose majesty Pharisees had quailed and slunk away. They laid His hands to rest, which had made the leper whole and given sight unto the

The Sorrowful Way

blind. They cleansed the blood from His wounded side, where John had once heard His heart beat with love to all mankind. Jesus, before whom death used to flee and give up his prey, was now Himself in the power of Death.

It pains us on first thought that the Body of the Lord should be hurriedly, and almost secretly, taken down from the Cross, on which He had triumphed gloriously, and hidden in a stranger's grave, for Whose burial no state and splendour had been too great; but on second thoughts the funeral of Jesus seems most becoming and worthy of His life. Modestly He entered the world, born of a village maiden, and cradled in the manger of an inn; lowly He began His work, baptised with Jerusalem sinners in the Jordan; meekly He taught and worked, who did not cry nor cause His voice to be heard in the streets: if He died in a public place in face of soldiers and priests and people, this was the one act in which He had no say, and now without show or pomp He must be buried. As He came so would He leave, in quietness and humility. And it were not right to think He had no honour at the last, for could anything be more perfect than the burial of Jesus. Were one desiring the best for his friend, would it be that his body should be carried

The Sorrowful Way

in a glittering carriage and laid in a grave which was never to be visited; should be followed by mourners who had regret on their faces, but no tears in their hearts? Or would it not be that, few or many, all that buried his friend should come for love's sake, and his epitaph be written on their hearts for ever? If this be so, then was our Master well buried, since love received His Body, love composed it after the agony, love wrapped it in spices and white linen, love carried it to the garden, love laid it in the tomb, love closed the door that He might sleep. No hireling, no stranger had anything to do with the burial of Jesus.

Companions of

The lowliness of Jesus was marvellous, and without limits, but it could not avail to hide Him from those who were watching for Him, either because they loved Him or because they hated Him. Unto His infancy gathered certain who were not many in number, but who were typical of His Church in heaven and on earth. There were the Holy Angels, who sang the Birth-Song of Bethlehem, and aged Simeon, who stood for the saints; there were the simple shepherds, of them who toil, and the wise men from the East, of them who are learned; there were Joseph and Mary, of them who were His family. Alas! there was also

The Sorrowful Way

Herod, who desired His life and the soldiers who slew His little brothers, the Holy Innocents. These all came, as it were, to His cradle, wherein He was unconscious, and paid their homage — or did Him such injury as they could. Unto His Cross, whereon He was stretched in death, friends and foes came as to His cradle. The soldiers came again, and they pierced His own heart now, which was already broken. There came unto that Cross also certain, in name of His Church, and did Him the last service, and the gathering at His Cross was still more honourable than the gathering at His cradle. Six persons, at least (and more may have been), united in the funeral of Jesus, and they fall into pairs, each of which had a special reason for their presence.

Two women of His blood, and the first was His mother, who in that hour has fully earned her title of Our Lady of Sorrows, and unto whom it is not wonderful that women of all ages have turned in their anguish. Never had any mother such privilege, never therefore had any such pain. When she presented her child in the temple Mary was told that a sword would pierce her heart, and she hardly possessed her child before the sword was seeking Him. He was a mystery to her in His

The Sorrowful Way

boyhood; in after years He went His own way, to her frequent dismay. During the days of His tribulation she suffered, with her Son; for every slander, insult, blow, found their last home in her heart, and when it came to the Cross, the nails went through her hands and feet, and the Virgin agonised beneath with her Son. A costly gift had He been to her, and yet of all women was she not most blessed of all, is she not most envied? What homage had been hers in the home of Nazareth, what obedience, thoughtfulness, comfort, and care in the days of her widowhood! What holy pride, what pure joy! What spiritual satisfaction in the after years, in spite of her motherly doubts and fears! One Son left no regret, one Son had fulfilled every hope, one Son had made a Galilean cottage into our Father's home, and His mother had come to bury Him.

The other woman of His kinsfolk, as we take it, was Salome, the sister of Mary, and the mother of John. Some families are coarse in blood, and the women thereof are passionate, evil-tempered, worldly; some are of fine blood, and their women are gentle-spirited, imaginative, and it was surely the purest stock in Israel which gave to the generation the mother of Jesus and the mother

The Sorrowful Way

of John. For Jesus Salome had waited, with Simeon and Anna and the saints, and in Jesus she had been satisfied; for Jesus Salome had prepared her son and in Him she had seen her son come to his height. When son and mother meet beside one Lord, sharing one faith and one love, religion has accomplished her perfect work, and the heart of Salome was filled with a sad gratitude to Jesus.

Two of the mourners were the conspicuous trophies of His grace, and could only be brought together by the Person of the Lord. Unto one art, with the spiritual instinct of her best days has, by the hand of Bartolommeo, Savonarola's friend, given the head of

Companions of

Jesus. John kneels and raises the dear helpless head, yet cannot endure the sight of the face. Once he had watched those lips, and every word which fell he had read in the light of those eyes; now those lips were silent and those eyes closed. He looks away with the countenance of one who has been cast out of heaven, and to whom the years henceforward would be laden with the sense of irreparable loss. For Jesus found this man, in his outward life a Galilean fisherman and in his inner being a natural saint, and He opened unto him the gates of vision, and John saw into the secret of all things, which is the heart of God. Unto the other

The Sorrowful Way

one of this pair the same art always assigns the feet of Jesus, for St. Mary Magdalene made these her own at Simon's feast. Again she bends her head, and her golden hair covers His feet: she cleanses them from the dust of death as once she did from the dust of the road, and mourns that His enemies have pierced His feet with nails, whose heart she pierced with her sin. A sinner, by the unchastened impulses of her rich passionate nature, she had wandered into strange places, and was stained with the mire of the streets, and Jesus had restored her to herself, redeeming a great passion, and consecrating it unto God.

Companions of

And two of the little company were of another order in society, and of another way in thought from the four. Nicodemus was a scholar and teacher of the law, a man of authority and learning, of candour also and an honest mind. After anxious reasoning and at a great sacrifice, this Rabbi became Jesus' disciple, and if he did not make open profession and attach himself to Jesus' personal following, let it be remembered that he never denied the Lord. Be it also remembered that when the council would have condemned Jesus untried and unheard, Nicodemus broke silence and pled for justice, and at last, when all had forsaken the Lord, this man's courage rose

The Sorrowful Way

to its highest, and his love burned clearest, and he came with spices for the Lord's body. Joseph of Arimathæa was of the class which, after the Pharisees, was the most inaccessible to Christ, for he was rich in goods and lived at ease. Very likely Jesus never knew him, and he had never said "Master" to Jesus; but the shrewd man of affairs had made his estimate of the young prophet, as he had made the same of Caiaphas. It was not in his power to save the noble enthusiast from the hands of the mob, for gold availeth not against fanaticism, but it could be his to see that after death Jesus should not be dishonoured. If the Master had not lived in rich men's houses in His life He should lie in a rich man's grave. The tomb which he had prepared for himself in his garden, Joseph gave without grudging to the Lord, and verily he had his reward. For the Master used Joseph's tomb three days, and then He left it open, with angels in His place. Blessed was the owner of Gethsemane, for in that garden Jesus drank His cup, but more blessed was Joseph, for in his garden Jesus rose from the dead and opened the gates of immortality. As the good man walked in his pleasaunce at eventide he would meditate on that empty grave, and one day he was laid there himself, where the Lord had lain, and the tomb was

The Sorrowful Way

to him the door into the Paradise of God.

And these were the six who buried the Master.

When they stood in the garden, having done what they could for the loved Body, their sorrow was not quite comfortless. His warfare was accomplished, and He could suffer no more. Never again would Pharisees insult Him, nor priests condemn Him, nor Judas betray Him, nor soldiers nail Him to the Cross. He rested at last beyond the reach of troubling, and God had given His Beloved sleep.

And this was the end of the Sorrowful Way.

www.ingramcontent.com/pod-product-compliance
Lightning Source LLC
Chambersburg PA
CBHW020256170426
43202CB00008B/389